Jerry Rice

Speedy Wide Receiver

SPORTS GREATS™

by

Thomas S. Owens

The Rosen Publishing Group's
PowerKids Press™
New York

Published in 1997 by The Rosen Publishing Group, Inc.
29 East 21st Street, New York, NY 10010

First Edition

Book Design: Kim Sonsky

Photo Credits: Cover © AP/Wide World Photos; p. 16 © Archive Photos; all other photos © AP/Wide World Photos.

Owens, Tom, 1960–
    Jerry Rice : speedy wide receiver / Thomas S. Owens.
        p.   cm. — (Sports greats)
    Includes index.
    Summary: Describes the life and achievements of the record-breaking wide receiver, from his childhood in Mississippi to his success with the San Francisco 49ers.
    ISBN 0-8239-5093-X
    1. Rice, Jerry—Juvenile literature. 2. Wide receivers (Football)—United States—Biography—Juvenile literature. 3. San Francisco 49ers (Football team)—Juvenile literature. [1. Rice, Jerry. 2. Football players. 3. Afro-Americans—Biography.] I. Title. II. Series: Sports greats (New York, NY)
GV939.R53094 1997
796.332'092—dc21
                                                                97-4151
                                                                    CIP
                                                                     AC

Manufactured in the United States of America

Contents

1	Made in Mississippi	5
2	He Had to Play	6
3	College Calls	9
4	Who Wants Rice?	10
5	Rice Is Real	13
6	Super Bowl or Rice Bowl?	14
7	Count on Jerry	17
8	Breaking Records	18
9	Future 49ers	21
10	On and Off the Field	22
	Glossary	23
	Index	24

Made in Mississippi

Jerry Rice was born on October 13, 1962, in the tiny town of Crawford, Mississippi. With five brothers and two sisters, Jerry's family didn't have much money. But it was a happy family. Jerry lived five miles from school. He learned to run the whole way. He became fast by chasing his neighbor's horses. If Jerry wanted to ride one of them, he'd chase it through the field and jump on its back.

Jerry's father was a bricklayer. Jerry helped his father build houses. He stood on a tall platform, catching the bricks his brothers passed to him. Jerry would one day use those same **skills** (SKILZ) to catch football passes.

Jerry's running and catching skills made him hard to stop on the field.

He Had to Play

Jerry was a fast runner. When Jerry was in tenth grade, the assistant principal saw how fast Jerry ran. One day, the assistant principal saw Jerry sneaking out of class. Jerry didn't want to be caught, so he ran away. He was fast, but he got caught.

The assistant principal knew Jerry's speed could be useful. He gave Jerry a choice: Be punished, or join the school's football team. Jerry chose football. He also decided to try basketball and track. Jerry was a good athlete in all three sports, but he liked football the best.

Jerry's speed helped make him a star football player. ▶

College Calls

Jerry had hoped to play for the large school near his hometown, Mississippi State College, but that team didn't want him. Instead, he played for the Delta Devils at Mississippi Valley State University, a small college in a small town. That was the only school that had **recruited** (ree-KREW-ted) him in high school.

As **wide receiver** (WYD ree-SEE-ver), Jerry scored 50 touchdowns in four seasons, setting eighteen different records. Jerry could have left and played for football teams at larger schools. But Jerry stayed, choosing the school that had chosen him.

Jerry knew that football was for him. He began setting records in college, and went on to set more records while playing for the National Football League (NFL).

9

Who Wants Rice?

In 1985, fifteen college players were chosen by the National Football League (NFL) teams as they took turns in the yearly **draft** (DRAFT). Two teams chose other players over Jerry. They weren't sure if Jerry's Delta Devils had played tough college teams. They wondered if Jerry would have been as good at a bigger college.

But the San Francisco 49ers wanted him on their team. And at the end of Jerry's first season, he hadn't let the 49ers down. He caught 49 passes and was named league **Rookie** (ROOH-kee) of the Year!

The 49ers knew they were lucky when they signed Jerry. He would help them become a winning team. ▶

Rice Is Real

After only one NFL season, football fans knew the player who wore the number 80 on his 49ers jersey. Jerry had won the wide receiver job from Freddie Solomon. Jerry's jersey number in college had been number 88. But that was Freddie's number, and he didn't want to give it up. So Jerry took the number 80.

Jerry had two nicknames, "Flash 80" and "World." "Flash 80" was because of his speed. "World" was the nickname he was given in college because he seemed to catch everything in the world!

During his second season, Jerry played in every game. He led the NFL with 86 **receptions** (ree-SEP-shunz). Only twice in football history had a receiver gained more than Jerry's 1,570 yards.

◀ Football fans across the country knew Jerry's number 80.

Super Bowl or Rice Bowl?

In Super Bowl XXIII (23), the 49ers beat the Cincinnati Bengals, 20 to 16, in front of 75,000 screaming fans. Jerry had a Super Bowl record gain of 215 yards.

Jerry's greatest play was the catch he never made. With 39 seconds left, two players for the Bengals headed for Jerry. They were worried that he'd catch another pass. The Bengals ignored Jerry's teammate, John Taylor. That left John free to catch the game-winning pass!

On that day, Jerry earned more than a **championship** (CHAMP-ee-un-ship) ring. He was named Most **Valuable** (VAL-yoo-bul) Player, or MVP, for the game too.

14

Jerry played so well that he was named MVP for his first Super Bowl. ▶

Count on Jerry

Jerry could do it all, and all the time. And his teammates, such as star quarterback Steve Young, knew it. For ten years in a row, Jerry never missed a game because of an **injury** (IN-jer-ee). Each year, he was chosen to start in the Pro Bowl, an **exhibition** (ex-ih-BISH-un) game of two teams made up of the NFL's top players. He caught at least one pass per game for more than 100 games in a row. Jerry's steady hands and dazzling moves could fool any team.

◀ The 49ers have a history of great players, including Steve Young and Jerry Rice.

17

Breaking Records

If people were ever unsure that Jerry was the greatest wide receiver in history, he changed their minds by the 1995 season. In 1994, Jerry broke the record for the most career touchdowns scored (140). Many people had thought this record would never be broken.

Jerry broke two more records in 1995. He had the most lifetime catches ever (940) and the most yards gained from receptions (14,004).

With each new season and game, Jerry pushes the **statistics** (stah-TISS-tiks) of his new records further out of the reach of other players.

18

Some of Jerry's records are so high that it will be difficult for other players to break them. ▶

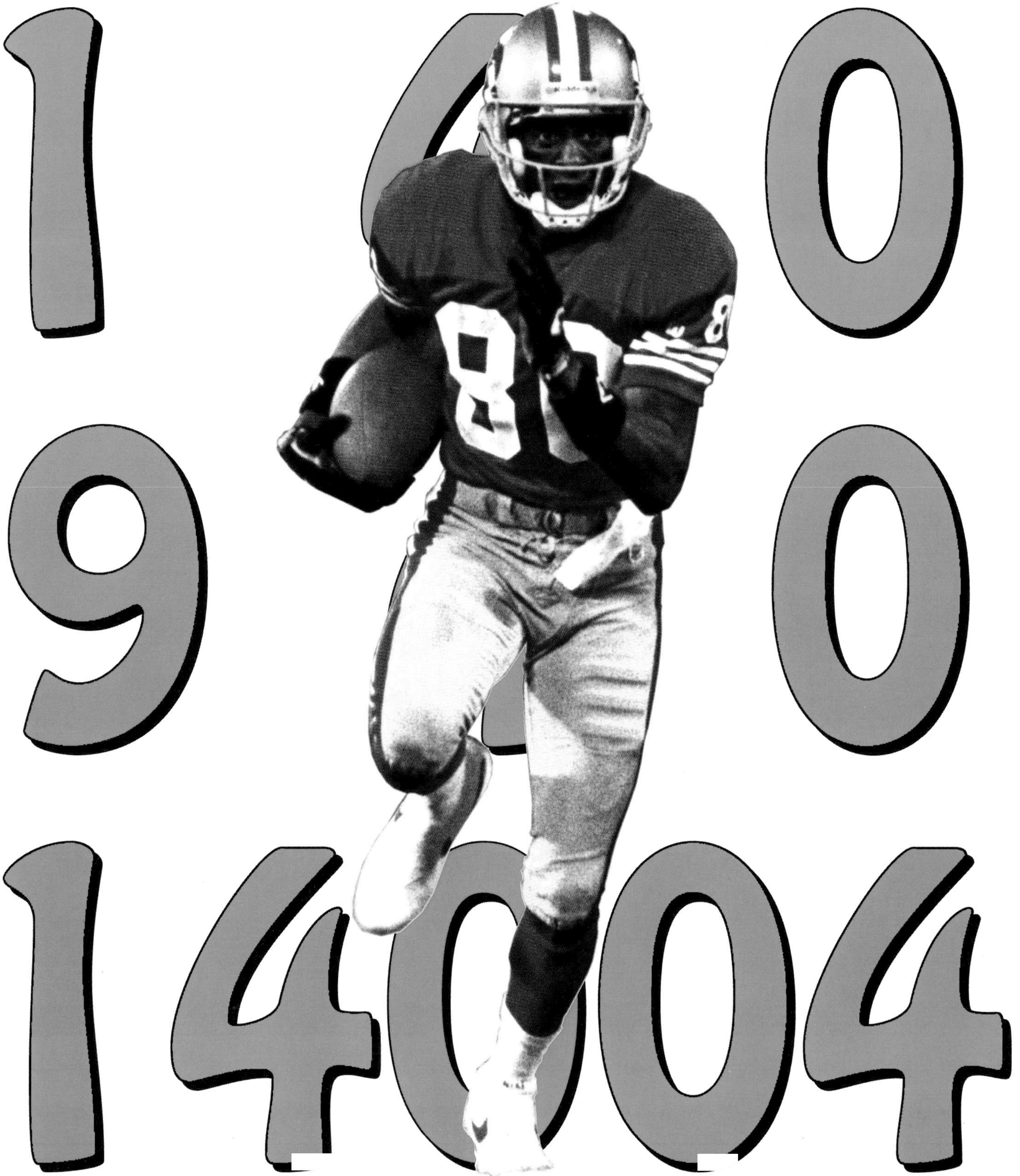
14004

Future 49ers

When Jerry first came to the 49ers in 1985, wide receiver Freddie Solomon knew the new player could take his job. But Freddie cared more about the team than being the star wide receiver. He played catch with Jerry after practices. Jerry remembered his kind teammate.

When J. J. Stokes joined the 49ers in 1995, and Iheanyi Uwaezuoke joined in 1996, Jerry knew these younger players might one day take *his* job. But Jerry helped the newcomers, letting them practice with him before the season started. Jerry, too, cared first about the team.

Jerry worked with players, such as J. J. Stokes, even though he knew J. J. might one day replace him as the star wide receiver.

On and Off the Field

Jerry looks good on and off the field. On the field, he keeps his helmet and shoes shiny, and sees that his jersey, socks, and shoulder pads are straight.

Out of uniform, Jerry likes to wear a diamond earring and the best suits. Jerry also likes to collect football cards. He's been pictured on more than 1,000 different cards!

Jerry married Jackie Mitchell, a friend from college. They have two daughters and a son. Jerry thanks more than teammates for his success. "My wife, my kids, and my parents have all been behind me, no matter what," he says. "That's a good feeling."

22

Glossary

championship (CHAMP-ee-un-ship) First place.

draft (DRAFT) A time during which professional teams take turns choosing new players from colleges, high schools, and other countries.

exhibition (ex-ih-BISH-un) A game for fun and show only. It is not part of the regular season.

injury (IN-jer-ee) When the body is hurt.

reception (ree-SEP-shun) The catch of a pass.

recruit (ree-KREWT) To get people to join something.

rookie (ROOH-kee) A first-year player.

skill (SKIL) The ability to do something.

statistic (stah-TISS-tik) A number that keeps track of the events of a game.

valuable (VAL-yoo-bul) Someone or something that is worth a lot to a team.

wide receiver (WYD ree-SEE-ver) A football position, when the player's main job is to catch passes.

Index

B
basketball, 6

C
championship, 14
Cincinnati Bengals, 14

D
Delta Devils, 9, 10
draft, 10

F
football cards, 22

M
Mississippi Valley State
    University, 9
Mitchell, Jackie, 22
Most Valuable Player
    (MVP), 14

N
National Football
    League (NFL), 10,
    13, 17
nicknames, 13

P
passes, 5, 10
Pro Bowl, 17

R
receptions, 13, 14, 18
records, 9, 14, 18
Rookie of the Year, 10

S
San Francisco 49ers,
    10, 14, 17, 21
Solomon, Freddie, 13,
    21
Stokes, J. J., 21
Super Bowl, 14

T
touchdowns, 9, 18
track, 6

U
Uwaezuoke, Iheanyi,
    21

W
wide receiver, 9, 13,
    18

Y
Young, Steve, 17